To: Jeremy
With love
Anne-Louise.
May 78.

NEW ZEALAND
Land of Scenic Contrast

Richard Silcock

NEW ZEALAND

Land of Scenic Contrast

Richard Silcock

Paul Hamlyn

Auckland, Sydney, London, New York, Toronto

Previous pages:
Moon over Mitre Peak, Milford Sound, Fiordland, South
Island

Tidal sandbank, Abel Tasman National Park, Nelson,
South Island

Right: Rocks, Kaikoura coast, Marlborough, South

Text: Conrad Bollinger

Design: Lindsay Missen

Editor: Clive Litt

Acknowledgements

The photographer wishes to express his grateful
thanks to the following for their assistance: Peter
Button, consultation on aerial photography; Tom
Hammond, Seddon sheep muster; Henning Pederson,
help and advice on Milford Sound; Mrs Fraser Smith,
help and advice on the West Coast; the Waimangu
Thermal Reserve, Rotorua; Tikitere Thermal Reserve,
Rotorua; Cape Kidnappers Sanctuary Trust, Napier;
Mission Vineyards, Taradale; and the Tourist Hotel
Corporation, Waitomo.

Published by Paul Hamlyn Ltd
Levien's Building
Cnr Airedale and St Paul Sts
Auckland

ISBN 0-600-07342-4
First Published 1974
Printed by McGraw-Hill
Far Eastern Publishers(S) Ltd.,
Singapore.

To Victoria

'What unknown affinity
Lies between mountain and sea
In a country crumpled like an unmade bed?'
DENIS GLOVER

'And whatever islands may be
Under or over the sea,
It is something different, something
Nobody counted on.'
ALLEN CURNOW

These are the elements that make up New Zealand: sea, mountains, rivers, farms, forests, rocks and sky. In their various forms and moods and combinations these things offer the supreme moments of scenic beauty which take New Zealanders far from their towns, and travellers thousands of kilometres over the sea, to gaze and wonder.

There are sights in New Zealand that have become obligatory for every package tour and every album of scenic photographs. But every one of these — Milford Sound, Mount Cook, Lake Manapouri, the Waitomo Caves, Pohutu Geyser, or the fern-lined shore of Ship Cove — justifies its reputation when seen and stored in the memory, or captured permanently by the lens of an imaginative cameraman.

Still, this country's renown for variety and contrast in the loveliness of its visual impact rests on much more than these favourite subjects for postcards. It rests on the distribution, throughout its 259,000 km² of landscape, of recurring combinations of disparate elements, placings together of pastureland and mountain, rock and sea, trees and sky, river and trees, mountains and lake . . . in an endless diversity.

It is perhaps no less remarkable that New Zealanders should be so frequently described as a colourless and conforming people, when they live against a backdrop of such manifold splendour. But a generation seems to be growing up, less absorbed with the abstractions of economic growth and statistical success and more concerned with the quality of life and environment, which may well alter the reputation of New Zealanders and bring their way of life into greater harmony with the reputation of the land they live in.

Previous page Upper slopes of Mount Egmont, Taranaki,
North Island

Below: Mustering sheep, Seddon, Marlborough, South Island

Below: Crack in hillside, Kawarau Gorge, Otago, South Island

Right: Sunset over Poverty Bay from Sponge Bay with Young Nick's Head on left, East Coast, North Island

Moments of more serene pleasure come from the sudden view of trees outlined against the sea. Once a land almost covered in forest, New Zealand still has many spots of shoreline where native bush reaches down to high watermark. Only a few native trees will stand up to the on-shore winds of our more exposed ocean coasts. One of the few is the hardy pohutukawa, known to the botanists as *Metrosideros excelsa*. A poet of the earliest pioneer generation, Alfred Domett, described these trees:

Stiff snaky writhing trunks, and roots that clave
And crawled to any hold the rampart gave.

In summer, the pohutukawa bursts into bright red flower, adding a sudden new colour contrast to the green and blue. For this reason the pioneers dubbed it the "New Zealand Christmas-tree". But the splash of red at the edge of the sea moved Fairburn to a more sober reflection:

In summer . . . the coasts
bear crimson bloom, sprinkled like blood
on the lintel of the land.

An island nation shows the image of its marine environment in its legends and traditions. Both the main constituent streams that have made the New Zealand people — Polynesian and British — originate from other islands with a heritage of dealings with the sea. According to the story passed down from the generations, the Maori came in a fleet of canoes from homelands further north in the Pacific. The Pakeha or white man made his entry in sailing ships, starting with the great explorers of the 17th and 18th centuries, followed in turn by sealers, whalers, traders, and from the 1830s by successive flotillas of immigrant ships.

The Maori legend of the country's origin makes the South Island the petrified remains of the giant canoe of the god-man hero Maui, and the North Island the great Leviathan that he hauled up from the depths of the sea. In its idealistic phases, Pakeha poetry has used the symbolism of the sea also. William Pember Reeves, politician and poet of the late Victorian era, described New Zealand's birth from the sea like that of Venus:

God girt her about with the surges
And winds of the masterless deep,
With tumult that rouses and urges
Quick billows to sparkle and leap.
He filled from the life of their motion
Her nostrils with breath of the sea,
And built her afar on the ocean
A citadel free.

The principal impact of this island nature has always been to make New Zealander's conscious of their distance from the rest of the world. Separated by over 1,600 kilometres of sea from the nearest landmass, they see the ocean as the dark, restless, potentially hostile element that divides her from the rest of humanity.

Always to islanders danger
Is what comes over the sea.

So wrote Allen Curnow in a poem inspired by the commemoration of the first meeting of Maori and European when Tasman's ships appeared off our coast in 1642. We are even inclined to see our lesser offshore islands as sentinels, keeping an outward watch. Alistair Campbell speaks like this about Kapiti, the wildlife sanctuary near the northern entrance to Cook Strait:

Massive, remote, familiar, hung with spray,
You seem to guard our coast, santuary
To our lost faith, as if against the day
Invisible danger drifts across the sea.

But the same sentiment might be addressed to the Brother Islands, or Great Barrier, or the Three Kings, or any of the well-known island landmarks that silhouette themselves on our coastal horizon.

Previous page: Ninety Mile Beach, Northland, North Island

Left: Monkey Bay, Marlborough, South Island

Below: Tutakaka Bay, Northland, North Island

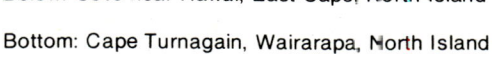

Left: Small headland, Abel Tasman National Park, Nelson, South Island

Below: Cove near Hawai, East Cape, North Island

Bottom: Cape Turnagain, Wairarapa, North Island

Below: Surf on a west coast beach near Auckland, North Island

Right: West Coast beach near Greymouth. West Coast, South Island

Left: Breaking surf near Piha, Auckland, North Island

Left: Rocky foreshore, Cape Egmont, Taranaki, North
Island

Below: Paekakariki coastline, Wellington, North Island

Left: Rock pools, Clifton, Hawke's Bay, North Island

Below: High tide, Farewell Spit, Nelson, South Island

Below: Brothers Island, Cook Strait

Right: Coastline at Matarangi, Coromandel Peninsula, North Island

Below: Shag Point north of Palmerston, Otago, South Island

Left: Moonlight on Queen Charlotte Sound, Marlborough
Sounds, South Island

Below: Tidal flats, West Richmond, Nelson, South Island

Below Cape Kidnappers, Hawke's Bay, North Island

Right Gannet, Black Reef Gannet Sanctuary, Hawke's Bay,
North Island

Right below: Gannets, Black Reef Gannet Sanctuary,
Hawke's Bay, North Island

Following page: Evening, Black Reef Gannet Sanctuary,
Hawke's Bay, North Island

'In this scarred country,
This cold threshold land
The mountains crouch like tigers.'
JAMES K. BAXTER

No other cluster of islands of comparable size can boast such lofty mountains as New Zealand. The Southern Alps, spinal mountain system of the South Island, have more than 200 named peaks which are 2,133 metres high. The principal ranges of the North Island (Raukumara, Huiarau, Ruahine, Tararua, Rimutaka) contain few peaks that top 1,675 metres; but of the four great volcanic cones in that island, one (Ruapehu) is over 2,750 metres (9,000 ft), and the other three (Egmont, Ngauruhoe, Tongariro) all exceed 1,830 metres (6,000 ft).

The highest point in the country is Mount Cook, 3,764 metres (12,349 ft), standing supreme among the Southern Alps above Lake Pukaki, 160 kilometres west of Christchurch. Its name honours the first European explorer to sight its lofty eminence from the coast on a clear day in 1769; but it retains also its ancient Maori name, Aorangi, usually translated as the piercer of heaven.

Perhaps the most noticeable feature of the New Zealand landscape is the impudent way these peaks intrude into the sky such a short horizontal distance from the vast flatness of the sea. Back in the 1890s, Pember Reeves referred to them as:
Peaks piercing the silence of heaven,
Snows gleaming in luminous space.

More recently, Charles Brasch has posed a question to the increasing numbers of people who pit their nerves and sinews against the stubborn and merciless intransigence of these mountains as a sport:

What have you seen on the summits, the peaks that plunge their
Icy heads into space? What draws you trembling
To blind altars of rock where man cannot linger
Even in death, where body grows light, and vision
Ranging those uninhabitable stations
Dazzled and emulous among the rage of summoning
Shadows and clouds, may lead you in an instant
Out from all footing?

Most prefer to admire them from afar, from the more congenial vantage points of flat land close to main roads, or the seats of passing aircraft. But however they are seen, close up or in the distance, in bright sunlight or shaded by clouds or night, these mountains form an imposing presence in the background of New Zealand life. Mount Cook is jostled by a number of peaks of only slightly lesser altitude. Mount Tasman and Mount Dampier are both over 3,350 metres (11,000 ft), and there are a dozen other mountains in the same area that exceed 3,050 metres (10,000). Individually they are impressive enough; collectively they present a massive symbol of the world's reach upward and outward, rivalling their more familiar namesakes in Europe.

The highest peaks of the North Island, being volcanic in origin, stand apart from the mountain ranges, and rise more dramatically from low-lying land. Mount Egmont stands isolated in the centre of Taranaki at the western extremity of the island. Most nearly a perfect cone, it is often compared with Japan's Fujiyama.

Ruapehu, Ngauruhoe, and Tongariro stand together in a National Park close to the centre of the island, not far to the south of Lake Taupo. Ruapehu and Ngauruhoe have both shown signs of volcanic activity in recent years, and they form part of a region of underground thermal activity which extends northwards through Wairakei and Rotorua to White Island.

New Zealand's mountain ranges still keep their mantle of native forest on their lower slopes. But the forest thins out, and the trees become more stunted, as one approaches the tops. Above the snow line, the trees enter into a convenient alliance with lesser forms of vegetable life, and develop protective beards of moss and lichen. But beyond a certain point they cannot grow, and snow-resistant tussock and occasional alpine flowers are the only living things that dare to make the open tops their home.

On the eastern and western sides of the Southern Alps there are a number of glaciers of spectacular extent. The Tasman Glacier on the eastern side, stretching down from the Mount Cook region, is the largest; but the most popular and accessible are the Fox and Franz Josef glaciers on the western side. Important to the economy of New Zealand as a tourist attraction, these glaciers have other uses: those on the eastern side feed rivers that are used to irrigate farmland and to generate electricity, and they help ensure a steady flow of water down these rivers throughout the year.

The mountains themselves are sometimes seen as wasteland, country that has no use. But they are the most visible manifestation of the elemental material out of which the whole country has been shaped.

In the course of breaking the country in for development, and especially at times like the gold-rushes of the last century when swarms of people were seeking for ways to cross from one side of the country to the other, the mountains offered a barrier to progress. Denis Glover has expressed the feeling which man has experienced at these times in a few simple lines:

When God made this place
He made mountains and fissures
Hostile, vicious, and turned
Away his face.

Today attitudes have changed. Now the eternal snows of Ruapehu and Egmont provide popular grounds for skiing in winter. In the South Island, favoured ski fields include Arthur's Pass in the Southern Alps, and Coronet Peak near Lake Wakatipu.

The mountains can still display their cruel hostility to mankind if they are not approached with sufficient respect. But forming as they do the backbone of these islands, they hold New Zealand together, combine with the sea to give it its unique character, and define its inward limits as the surrounding sea defines its outward ones.

Previous page: Snow-covered alpine tussock near Mount Cook, Canterbury, South Island

Left: The Southern Alps from the west showing Mount Cook (left) and Mount Tasman, South Island

Below: Morning mist, Mount Sefton and the Footstool, Southern Alps, South Island

Below: The Lindis Pass Saddle, Otago, South Island

Right: Slopes of the Wakefield spur, from near The Hermitage, Mount Cook, Southern Alps, South Island

Right below: The Remarkables near Queenstown, Otago, South Island

Below: Mount Turiwhate from Wainihinihi, West Coast, South Island

Right: Looking over rolling farmland to Mount Ruapehu, Waiouru, North Island

Right: Sunset over Mount Ben Cruachan, Otago, South Island

Left: Mount Cook, Southern Alps. Showing from left, Harper Saddle, St David's Dome, Mount Dampier, and the long summit ridge of Mount Cook with its three peaks, South Island

Below: Snow on Coronet Peak, Queenstown, Otago, South Island

Below: Red Soil, Whangapoua, Coromandel Peninsula, South Island

Following page: Mount Tasman (3,498 m, 11,475 ft) to the left and Mount Cook from the West Coast, South Island

Far Left: Mount Egmont (8,260 ft) Taranaki, North Island

Left: Mount Christina, Hollyford Valley, Fiordland, South Island

Below: Valley near the Ailsa Mountains, Fiordland, South Island

Below: Mount Ngauruhoe erupting January 22 1974,
Volcanic Plateau, North Island

Right: Ice fractures on the upper Franz Joseph Glacier, West
Coast, South Island

For the size of the country they drain, New Zealand's rivers are impressive in number and variety, and many are of considerable volume and length.

The Waikato River, which takes the overflow of Lake Taupo in the central high country of the North Island, winds for more than 321 kilometres through a variegated landscape before it finds the Tasman Sea 32 kilometres south of the entrance to Manukau Harbour. On the way it supplies the driving force for a chain of more than half a dozen hydroelectric power-stations, and water for several large towns as well as some of the richest dairy pasture in the country.

The Rangitikei, 209 kilometres long, flows through another of the North Island's prosperous farming districts, but its upper reaches, like those of the Wanganui, are among rugged bush-clad hills. The Wanganui has its source on the slopes of one of the· volcanic mountains near the centre of the island; the Rangitikei springs from the Kaimanawa Range not many miles to the east.

Variety is added to the river scenery offered in the North Island by the more slowly-flowing stretches of rivers which join the sea across the flatter coastal plains, or in the tidal creeks and inlets of Northland. In the area of thermal activity around Wairakei and Rotorua, there are also a number of streams whose waters are heated to uncomfortable temperatures, but these are soon cooled by distance or by joining the chiller waters of larger streams and lakes.

The typical North Island river has been described as "brown-running, stoney and swift, carving its way through hills bushed or cleared, swelling dangerously with spring anger, but always in a hurry to great the ocean".

The South Island's rivers display an equal variety of scenic attractions. The Southern Alps shed their water in both directions, but the rivers that flow east across the Canterbury Plains and through the hills of Otago are both longer and larger than those that make the briefer and steeper distance to the Tasman Sea on the West Coast side.

The Clutha River, which carries a greater volume of water than any other river in the country, flows from Lake Wanaka and Lake Hawea nearly 320 kilometres to the Pacific Ocean 80 kilometres south of Dunedin. As well as offering majestic scenic views, this river also feeds several hydro stations in use or projected, and is largely tapped to irrigate the orchards of Central Otago.

"Land of mountains and running water" was A. R. D. Fairburn's apt summing-up of New Zealand, and the two features are often seen together. Among the rivers which flow directly from the mountains into the southern lakes, the Dart and Rees rivers which feed Lake Wakatipu have especially splendid alpine settings — though the mountains here about, the Humboldt, Richardson, and Harris ranges, are strictly separate from the Southern Alps. Flowing through ancient glacial valleys with steep sides and comparatively wide floors, these rivers look up across lower slopes clad in beech and other native forest trees to towering peaks covered with perpetual snow.

On the West Coast of the South Island, the rivers tend to be more fast-flowing, and the gorges of the Otira and Buller furnish grandly untamed settings for the rivers that rush through them. On this side of the South Island, with its sharp drop from the mountains to the sea, there is more than one notably impressive waterfall. The Bowen Falls in Milford Sound have a beauty all their own, and the Sutherland Falls, dropping in a series of broken leaps a sheer 680 metres (1,904 ft), are among the highest in the world. But New Zealand's steep and irregular terrain ensures spectacular falls on rivers throughout the country. For volume and sound, the Huka Falls and the Aratiatia Rapids. not far from one another on the Waikato near its starting point at the outlet of Lake Taupo, are spectacular indeed, although the flow over the Huka Falls is now controlled in the interests of power generation.

Among the great rivers of Canterbury, the Rakaia and the Waimakariri are typical. Thundering out of mountain gorges, they gradually lose pace as they gain volume across the plains, swinging from side to side on wide stony beds. After heavy rains and in the spring thaw, however, the bulk of water in these rivers increases dramatically, and the breadth of their beds and the strenuous control measures adopted in recent decades have done much to overcome their rampages.

It was the rivers of the South Island that were the chief Mecca of the New Zealand gold rushes in the 1860s. The extensive alluvial gold deposits discovered in Otago, Nelson and West Coast rivers particularly played a significant part in the economic development of the country — among other reasons, for the vast and heterogeneous swarm of immigrants that it attracted from across the world. A single gold dredge still collects a small but profitable quantity of gold from one of these rivers, and an ageing and diminishing group of prospectors still sift gravel on these riverbeds in old-fashioned pans.

But the principal attraction of these rivers today lies in the scenery to which they so signally contribute — although freshwater fishing, chiefly for trout, brings many visitors.

Previous page: Rock formation, Clutha River, Otago, South Island

Right: Otira River, West Coast, South Island

Below: Mouth of the Tongaporutu River, Taranaki, North Island

Below: Rocky bed of a tributary of the Cobb River, Nelson, South Island

Below: Sutherland Falls, Lake Kaniere, West Coast, South Island

Below: Sutherland Falls, Fiordland, South Island

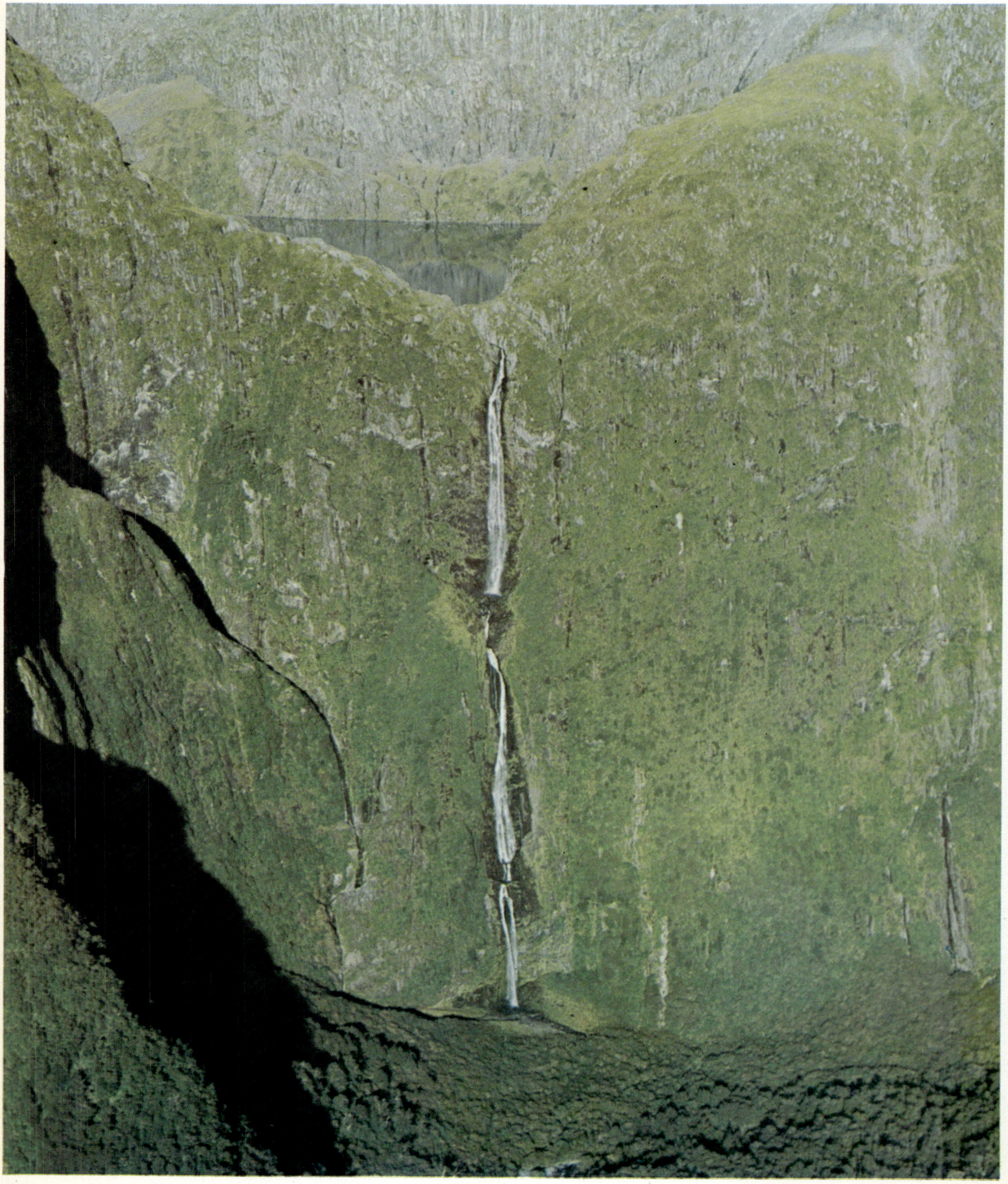

Below: Bowen Falls, Milford Sound, Fiordland, South Island

Left: Upper Bowen Falls, Milford Sound, Fiordland, South
Island

Below: Waimakariri River, looking towards Arthur's Pass,
Canterbury, South Island

Right: Matakitaki River near Murchison, Nelson, North Island

Below: Rangitikei River from Vinegar Hill, Rangitikei, North Island

Following Page: Wairoa River, Bay of Plenty, North Island

Left: Mouth of the Waikato River, South Auckland, North Island

Below: Small tributary of the Makaroa River, Haast Pass, West Coast, South Island

Below: Bridal Veil Falls, Waikato, North Island

Bottom: One of the many small tributaries of the upper
Wanganui River, King Country, North Island

Right: Junction of the Hanmer and Waiau rivers south of Hanmer, Canterbury, South Island

Below: Thermal stream at Waimangu, Rotorua, North Island

Left: Boil the Billy Creek on Cattle Flat, Matukituki Valley,
West Coast, South Island

Below: Hutt River, Wellington, North Island

'Man's earth: is it not now
Man's marked with the sign of axe and plough,
Watered, shaded, settled?'
CHARLES BRASCH

Next to its scenery, New Zealand is probably best known in the world for its primary produce — especially butter, meat, wool, cheese, and apples.

Before European settlement began, the Maori engaged in a simple kind of agriculture, growing food crops (chiefly the sweet potato, *kumara*) in level plots close to their villages. With the overwhelming of the Maori way of life by the mass Pakeha immigration of the last century, most Maori land was alienated, and nearly all the useable tracts between the mountains and the sea gradually taken over and used for growing crops or pasturing stock.

Crop farming occupies comparatively little of New Zealand's farmland today. Wheat is still grown on much of the Canterbury Plains, and there are extensive orchards in Nelson and Hawke's Bay, and (especially for stone fruit) in Central Otago. A growing wine industry derives from grapes grown in Hawke's Bay, Poverty Bay, Waikato, Auckland and the more northern parts of the North Island, and hops and tobacco grow readily around Nelson at the northern end of the South Island. There are also wide areas of market garden on flat land, especially within easy access of the main centres of population.

The greater part of New Zealand farming is concerned with raising sheep and cows, and as a general rule the wetter areas on the western side of the country favour the cows, while sheep flourish better on the drier land to the east. Hill country farming in both islands is mainly confined to the pasturing of sheep.

Traditional patterns have made dairy farms smaller units, often 40 hectares and less, while sheep stations have frequently extended to several thousands of hectares. Difficulties with longstanding overseas markets have recently undermined confidence in the dairy industry, and more dairy farmers are said to be raising cattle for beef.

Sheep farmers have always produced for both the wool and meat markets. Mutton has been a staple export of New Zealand along with dairy produce ever since the introduction of refrigeration to the holds of ships a century ago.

New Zealand's farm lands present marked contrasts to the scenery of mountain, forest and sea. Here the wilderness has been subdued, and the hand of man is everywhere apparent in roads, bridges, fences, and dams. Typical farm buildings are the concrete milking shed of the dairy districts, and in sheep country the vast bulk of the woolshed, traditionally painted brick-red, surrounded by holding pens. But smaller and shabbier sheds are still to be seen on less prosperous back-country farms — shabbier, but no less picturesque.

The process of subduing this land was tough enough. Blanche Edith Baughan, a New Zealand poet and writer of the Edwardian period with an abiding interest in the differences and similarities between her adopted country and her native England, once wrote in the *persona* of a pioneer farmer:

Ay, the Fire went through and the Bush has departed, the green Bush departed, green Clearing is not yet come.
'Tis a silent, skeleton world.

And there are still remote areas where the charred remains of tall timber stand among the sheep on the hillsides like the ghosts of the forest that has passed away.

But much of the farm land shows no sign of having ever been anything other than farm land. In the words of B. E. Baughan's farmer again:

That bit o' Bush paddock I fall'd myself, an' watch'd, eacy year, come clean
Don't it look fresh in the tawny? A scrap of Old-country-green?

To approach the natural world of mountain and forest, trampers often have to cross farm fields from the nearest roadhead. Undoubtedly the open country has its own attractions, and there are outdoor men who prefer wandering over the gentler folds of farmland to clambering up the sides of mountains, and wide vistas of grazing hillsides to the enclosed greenness of the bush. Fairburn expressed this preference in a passage which evokes a typical stretch of New Zealand upland sheep country:

I could be happy, in blue and fortunate weather, roaming the country that lies between you and the sun,
over the hills, fold after fold,
following the gradual sheeptracks, winding slowly past gullies flecked with the ragwort curse or golden with the uneconomic gorse.

But the farmers, who have to tramp these hills for a living, probably derive as little pleasure from it as they do from the sight of the ragwart and the gorse — visually pleasing to the idle visitor, but a continual enemy to the economics of farming.

There are wide areas (in the Manawatu, for instance, and parts of Canterbury) where the landscape looks much like that of farm land anywhere else. But as soon as you approach hilly country, or lift your eyes to the backdrop of high country that's never far away in New Zealand, you realise that New Zealand farms have scenic advantages which are unique.

Left: Ewe and lamb on the Canterbury Plains, mid-winter, Canterbury, South Island

Far Left: Sheep Station — Lake Wanaka, Otago South Island

Below: Farmland near Ashhurst. Manawatu, North Island

Right: Mission Vineyards, Taradale, Hawke's Bay, North Island

Bottom Right: Farmland near Kawhatau, Rangitikei, North Island

Below: Sheep Country, Tarata, Taranaki, North Island

Right: Winter-feed crop with outliers of the Seaward Kaikouras in the background, Marlborough, South Island

Bottom Right: Rolling farmland, Lake Tiniroto, Hawke's Bay, North Island

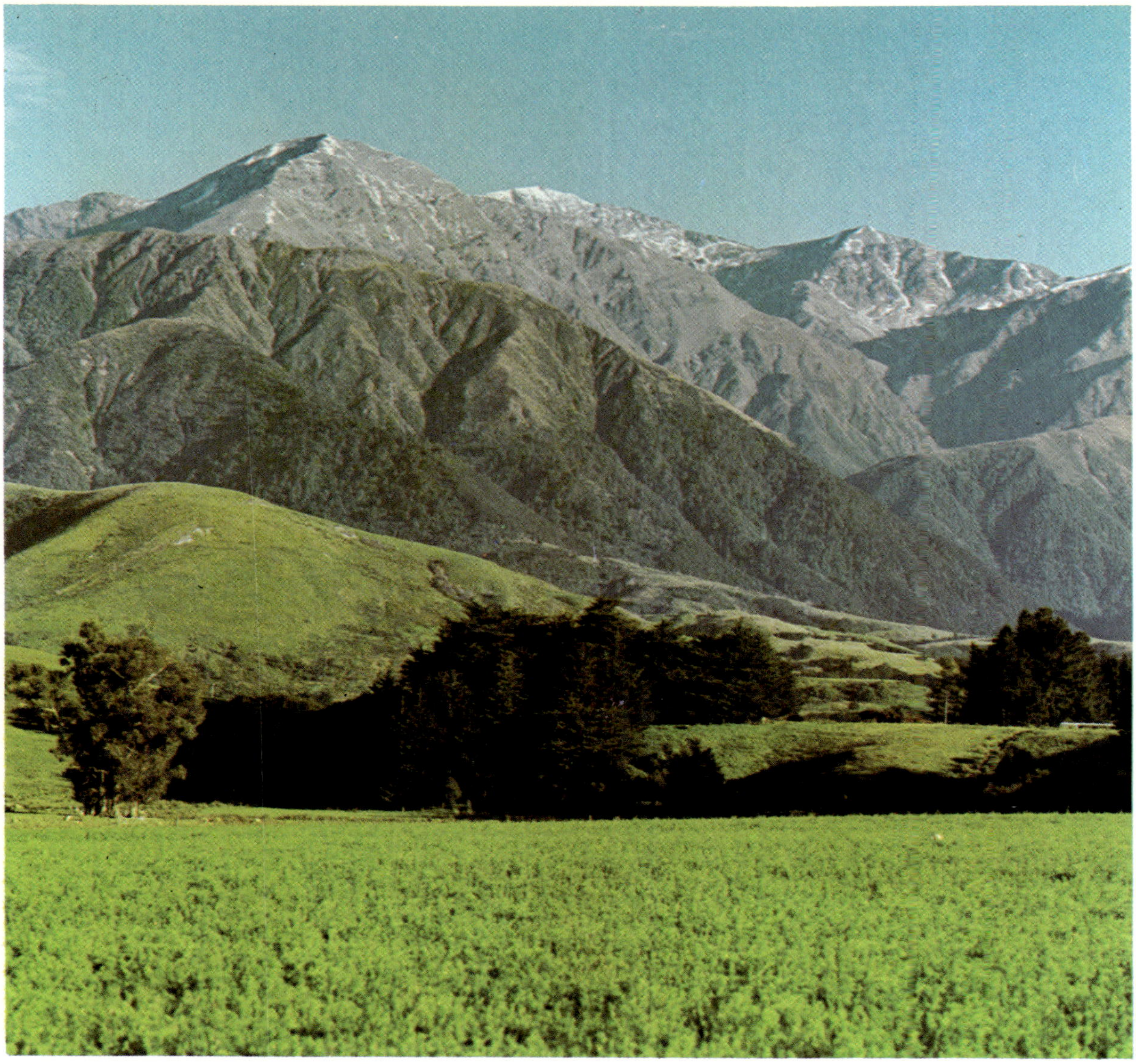

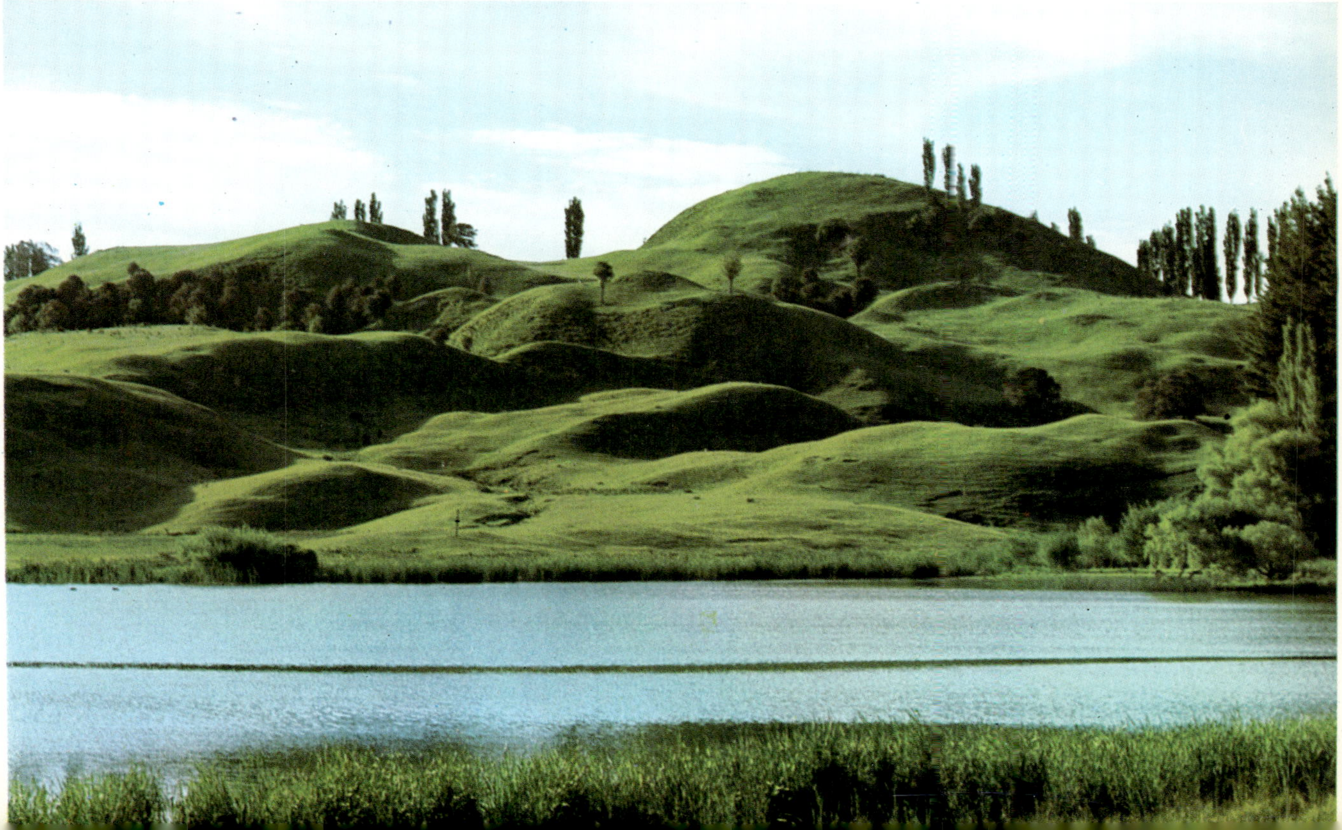

Right: Market gardening near Outram, Otago, South Island

Below: Coastal farmland, Foveaux Strat near Bluff, Southland, South Island

Right: Mixed farming near Nukumaru, Wanganui, North Island

Left: Coastal farm on the Coromandel Peninsula, North Island

Below: farmland north of Linton, Manawatu, North Island

Bottom: Poor pastures near Te Paki, Northland, North Island

Below: Rain over farmland near Clifden, Southland, South Island

Right: Dairy country near Te Awamutu, Waikato, North Island

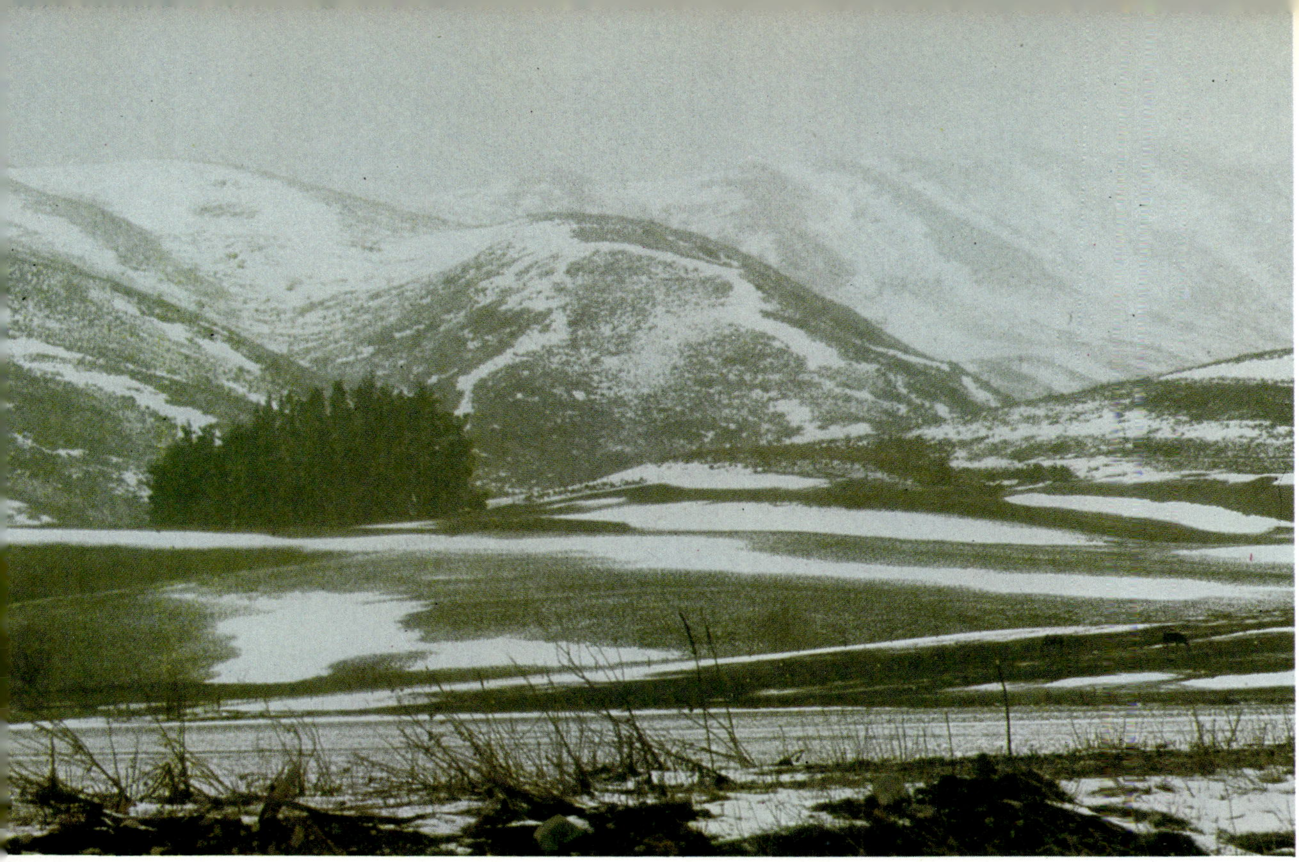

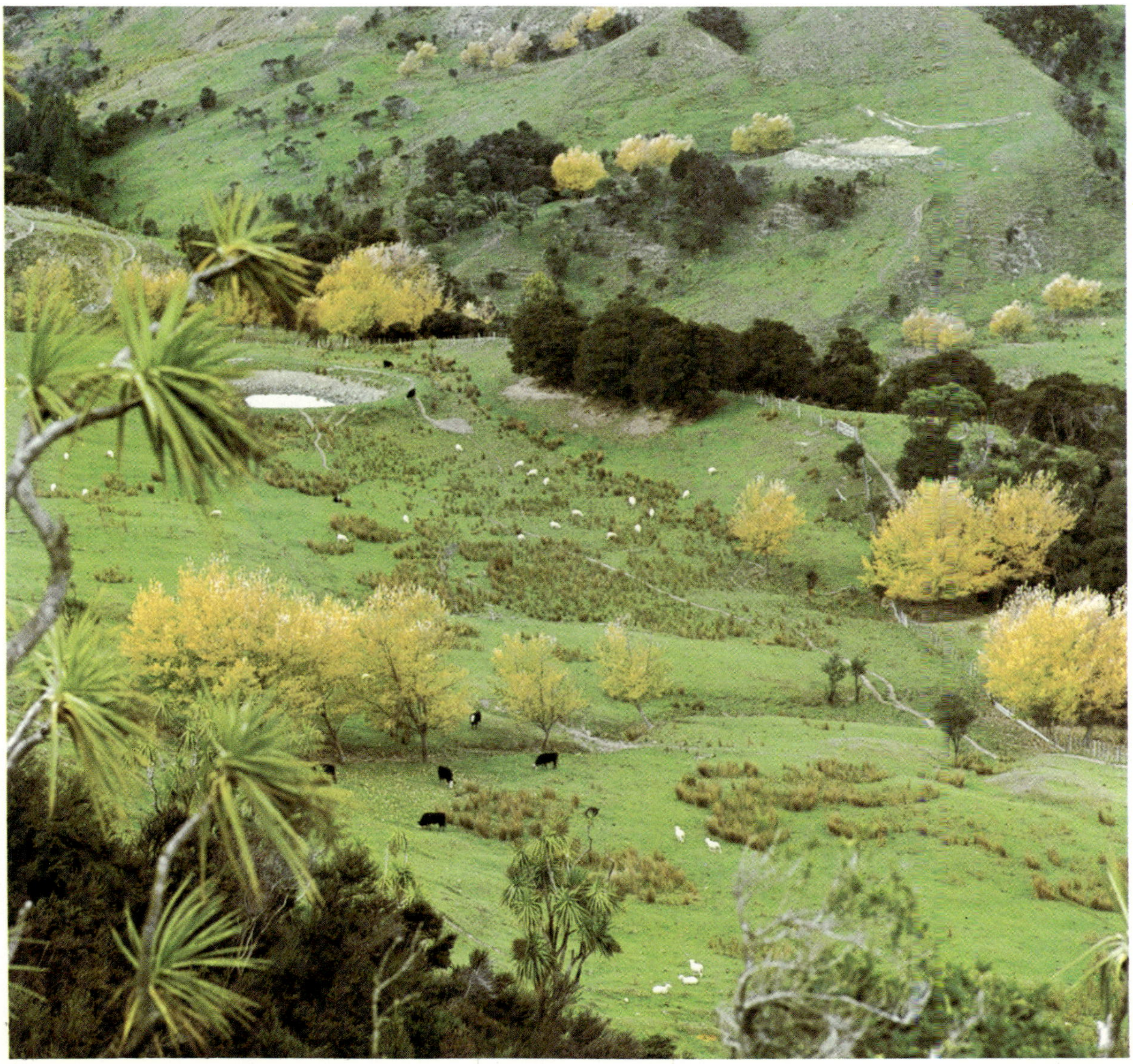

Below: Buttercups, Cheviot, Canterbury, South Island

Below: Drought-stricken farmland south of Seddon, Marlborough, South Island

Right: Ploughed fields, Cheviot, Canterbury, North Island

Below: Hop vines, Motueka, Nelson, South Island

Bottom: Cox's Orange apples, Appleby, Nelson, South Island

Below: Farmland near Masterton, Wairarapa, North Island

Left: Coastal dairy farmland near Oakura, Taranaki, North Island

'Let them be smooth and sweet as all those
morning lakes,
Yet active and leaping, like fish the fisherman
takes;
And strong as the dark deep-rooted hills, strong
As twilight hours over Lake Wakatipu are long.'
DENIS GLOVER

Not unnaturally, a country of many mountains and many rivers is also a country of many lakes. And if running water has charms of its own, then so has still water — especially when it gives back the reflection of scenically beautiful surroundings.

The larger lakes of the South Island — Tokapo, Pukaki, Wanaka, Hawea, Te Anau, Manapouri, and Wakatipu — lie in old glacial valleys among the foothills of the Southern Alps and the lesser ranges that radiate out from the southern end of the Alps. And their beauty is intensified by the grandeur of their surroundings.

Situated at high altitudes, far inland, and away from main centres of population and trunk roads, these lakes have never served (as the Great Lakes of North America have) as major communication routes and only rarely as a means of opening up new hinterlands. With the use of South Island rivers for electric power generation since World War I these lakes have assumed an increasing economic importance as holding reservoirs. The latest lake to take on this role was Manapouri, and the resultant plans to vary its water level to meet power requirements brought such a massive public reaction that the very name of this lake has become a symbol of the movement for the preservation of New Zealand's natural environment.

North Island lakes have also become important as reservoirs for the generation of electric power in the rivers that flow from them. Lake Taupo, the biggest lake in the country (606 km²), has gained added national attention in recent years for this reason, and its level from day to day is a matter of public comment during periods of power shortage in early winter months. Since the development of a series of hydro-stations near its point of outlet in the 1940s, the fluctuations of Lake Waikaremoana have resulted in some damage to the beauty of its shoreline despite efforts to conserve and restore it.

Partial compensation for this kind of spoliation has been offered by the development of artificial lakes in connection with hydro schemes on the Waikato River. These have proved popular resorts for certain aquatic sports, but have yet to establish themselves as scenic attractions comparable with the lakes created by nature. Artificial lakes have, however, been traditional points of scenic beauty in public parks and gardens. Supreme in this category is Wanganui's Virginia Lake.

Like their adjacent rivers, many of the North Island's lakes are well stocked with trout, and the pursuit of this appetising game has added another attraction to those associated with their visual beauty.

The best known lakes of the North Island, situated on a volcanic plateau, derive much of their interest from the thermal activity that is to be found near them. But parts of the shores of Lake Taupo and Lake Waikaremoana are distinguished by their magnificent forest settings. In this respect they compare with Te Anau and Manapouri in the South Island, and some of the smaller lakes of inland Nelson and Westland.

Lake Rotorua, in the midst of the North Island's most popular tourist resort and thermal playground, is extremely picturesque, but has become a major problem because of its widespread use as a sump for sewage. Lesser lakes in the vicinity, such as Rotoehu, Rotoiti, Rotomahana, and Tarawera, continue to display their attractions in more virgin form.

Tarawera, formed in forest country as a result of a major volcanic eruption less than a century ago, holds within its depths a one time scenic splendour of the world — the famous Pink and White Terraces.

Maori legends attach to nearly all these lakes, but the most famous is surely that of the maiden Hinemoa and how she swam from the island on Lake Rotorua to the mainland to elope with her lover Tutanekai in defiance of the wishes of her family. Maori maiden swimmers abound in the traditional stores of lakeside and seacoast: Hawke's Bay Maoris tell the story of Pania of the Reef, and there is a similar story of a girl swimming from Kapiti Island to what is now Wellington's "golden coast". But the story of Hinemoa is the prototype of them all. From this charming legend derives the popular Maori song "Pokarekare".

Apart from its larger and better known lakes, New Zealand has hundreds of smaller and lesser-known stretches of standing water which are no less compellingly beautiful. Among the mountains, the smallest tarns take on an ethereally fairy quality from the way in which they reflect the peaks that stand about them and the moods of the sky above.

Previous Page: Lake Manapouri with Stoney Point in the foreground, Pomona Island and the Kepler Mountains in the distance, Fiordland, South Island

Left: Horseshoe Bay, Lake Waikaremoana, Urewera, East Coast, North Island

Below: Early morning, Lake Taupo, Volcanic Plateau, North Island

Below: Western shore of Lake Taupo, Volcanic Plateau, North Island

Right: Lake Pukaki in late-afternoon sun with the Ben Ohau Range in the background, Canterbury, South Island

Below: Morning mist shrounds a small island, Lake Taupo, Volcanic Plateau, North Island

Bottom: Later afternoon sun on the Remarkables with Queenstown in the foreground, Lake Wakatipu, Otago, South Island

Below: Western shore of Lake Pukaki, Mackenzie Country, Canterbury, South Island

Right: Thermal lake at Waimangu, Rotorua, North Island

Right below: Small lake near Denniston, Mount Rochfort Plateau, West Coast, South Island

Left: Lake Mapourika with the Southern Alps in the distance,
West Coast, South Island

Below: Lake Hayes, Otago, South Island

Right: Sunset over Lake Kaniere, West Coast, South Island

Below: Lake Rotoehu with tree ferns in the foreground, Rotorua, North Island

Bottom: Lake Tekapo, Canterbury, South Island

Left: Lake Tekapo in the Mackenzie Country, Canterbury, South Island

Below: Lake Wanaka with Ruby Island in the foreground, Otago, South Island

Below: Lily pads, Lake Virginia, Wanganui, North Island

'Gone is the forest's labyrinth of life,
It's clambering, thrusting, clasping, throttling race,
Creeper with creeper, bush with bush at strife,
Struggling in silence for a breathing space;
Below, a realm of tangled rankness rife,
Aloft, three columns in victorious grace.'
WILLIAM PEMBER REEVES

Writing at the turn of the present century, the poet Reeves deplored the passing of the dense rain forest that once covered most of New Zealand. Still, despite continued inroads in the name of economic development, much of that forest remains in national parks and the less accessible foothills of the ranges; and in reserve areas and other places where it has been left alone, cleared land has slowly cloaked itself again in a second growth of native bush.

Fiordland in the far south offers some of the most beautiful forest scenery, partly because the original vegetation has been least disturbed there, partly because of the way it combines with craggy peaks, and still and falling water, to present a picture of wild beauty rivalling the most romantic conception of the lost world of Eden.

The forest held a central importance in the economics of the Maori before the days of Pakeha settlement. There he hunted the kereru (or wood pigeon) and other large songbirds whose flesh provided a staple meat element in the diet of inland tribes and many coastal dwellers at certain times of the year. After due obeisance to the forest god Tane, he felled the timber to make his houses, food stores, palisades and canoes.

The coming of the white man changed the nature and pace of these activities. Beginning with the release of the European pig in the forests of both islands by Cook's expedition of 1773, a variety of exotic mammals have made their home there, including goats, Australian opossums, and several species of deer. Deer, pigs, and to a lesser extent goats, are favourite game for huntsmen, while all native birds now have legislative protection. The introduced mammals are now recognised as an active threat to native forests, and control of their numbers is encouraged by the authorities.

Depredation of the timber also began in a big way with the trade in hardwood trunks (chiefly the native conifers, kauri, totara and matai) for ships' spars at the turn of the 19th century. And from the time of large-scale white settlement, the clearing of the forest became a general prelude to the conversion of the country to European-style farming, as well as the basis of a milling industry which provided the principal material for building New Zealand homes until the 1950s.

These developments have been accompanied by the massive introduction of exotic trees. Faster growing, these have usually proved more economic for providing shelter on farms as well as for mass planting for timber. Shelter belts of *pinus insignis* and macrocarpa and stands of poplar, willow and Australian blue gum have become as familiar on the New Zealand landscape as any of our native trees, their presence emphasizing the bicultural nature of the country.

Since the 1930s, private and State organisations have planted extensive forests of exotic trees, especially North American pines, for eventual milling for timber, paper pulp and other commercial uses. The largest exotic plantations are in the Golden Downs region south of Nelson, and the Kaingaroa and Tokoroa areas between the Rangitaiki and Waikato Rivers in the vicinity of Rotorua.

Trees native to other lands have also been planted extensively for decorative purposes in our cities, in private and public gardens, and along the footpaths of wider streets. But some of the most decorative of introduced *flora* are highly controversial because their aesthetic qualities conflict sharply with their role in the economy. Gorse and blackberry, for instance, which enrich the colour of our hillsides in season, spread rapidly to take command of the land, and are notoriously difficult to eradicate.

The native forests of New Zealand form a strong contrast to the open woodland of Britain and northern Europe. The thick undergrowth, the prevalence of ferns and creepers, the almost universally evergreen nature of the trees, and the number with broad, thick, shiny leaves, all combine to give the New Zealand bush the qualities which a visitor from overseas associates with the word ''jungle''

One native tree that tends to grow in more open woodland style is the beech (genus *Nothofagus),* which grows in a variety of species mainly on the lower mountain slopes of both islands. Bitter public debate has surrounded Government proposals to exploit the more accessible beech forests of Westland commercially.

Among the best-known New Zealand trees are the tree ferns, especially the ponga, the silver underside of whose leaf has been stylistically represented as a national symbol. Often found in large numbers standing together at the edge of the forest, or along the sides of streams, these strangely primitive trees filter the light through their delicately-shaped fronds in a most picturesque way. And their uniformed fronds have evoked the weirdest associations. Fairburn once wrote:

Observe the young and tender frond
Of this punga: shaped and curved
Like the scroll of a fiddle: fit instrument
To play archaic tunes.

Along the coasts, the most colourful sight is the pohutukawa, but there are several species of *coprosma,* especially the taupata, that stand up well to the coastal weather; and the swampy edges of many Northland tidal estuaries are thick with stands of mangrove, or manawa as the Maori call it.

Like the coasts, the mountains of New Zealand also have a characteristic vegetation of their own. Stunted bushes, tussock plants, and leathery-leaved shrubs cling close to the ground and resist the chill blasts of winter. In summer, alpine lilies and daisies burst from the edge or rocks.

There are still plenty of areas of native growth, ensuring the survival of most of the almost innumerable species of native plant life classified with such care and wonder by the botanists of the past. But many of them are now remote enough from the setting of most New Zealanders' lives to ensure that they have to travel far and deliberately to catch a glimpse of the kind of place their whole country was less than 200 years ago. And it is hard not to sympathise with the sentiment of Pember Reeves' somewhat Victorian lament for

The ravaged beauty God alone could plan,
And builds not twice! A bitter price to pay
Is this for progress — beauty swept away!

Previous page: Beech trees in the Eglinton Valley, Fiordland, South Island

Right: Pohutukawa tree, Matarangi Beach near Whangapoua, Coromandel Peninsula, North Island

Below: Pohutukawa blossoms, Coromandel Peninsula, North Island

Left: Eucalyptus trees and crop fields, Marlborough, South Island

Right: Morning mist rises over forest near Westport, West Coast, South Island

Below: Beech forest, Lewis Pass, linking Canterbury and West Coast, South Island

Below: Snow-covered trees in the Haast Pass area, West Coast, South Island

Below: Exotic pine forest near Tokoroa, Volcanic Plateau,
North Island

Right: Tree ferns, Takaka, Nelson, South Island

Below: Stunted trees, Waitangi-Taona River valley, West Coast, South Island

Below: Autumn populars at Otoko near Parapara, Wanganui, North Island

Bottom: Gorse-filled gully, Otago, South Island

Right: Matagouri and other scrub covered with snow near Mount Cook, Canterbury, South Island

Below: Snow on alpine vegetation near Mount Cook, Canterbury, South Island

Bottom: Late-afternoon sun and mist near Tokoroa, Volcanic Plateau, North Island

Left: Sunset over tidal mangrove swamps, Coromandel, North Island

Below: Lush rainforest in the Milford Sound, Fiordland, South Island

Left: Bright green shoots of new vegetation in dense native forest, Milford Sound, Fiordland, South Island

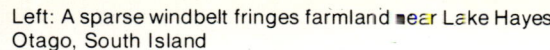

Left: A sparse windbelt fringes farmland near Lake Hayes, Otago, South Island

'These islands:
The remnant peaks of a lost continent,
roof of the world, molten droppings
from earth's bowels, gone cold;
ribbed with rock, resisting the sea's corrosion
for an age, and an age to come.*

A. R. D. FAIRBURN

The antiquity of New Zealand is affirmed by more than its unique plant life and the absence of native animal life other than birds — some of them of curiously primitive species. The very shape and substance of the land itself links it more dramatically with the prehistoric world than most parts of the earth's cooling crust.

The geysers, mud pools and hot streams of the Rotorua region reveal the proximity of the underground pressures associated with the planet's central core. So do the still occasionally active volcanoes of the central North Island, and the steam holes that have been tapped for the generation of electricity at Wairakei.

But elsewhere, where thermal activity has long since ceased, the land has been left twisted into weird patterns that serve as a constant reminder of its primitive origins.

Rock outcrops often dominate the skyline — noticeably at certain points along the coast, but also in many areas far inland. The Punakaiki Rocks on the West Coast north of Greymouth are often visited, but equally impressive are the Pinnacles near Cape Palliser at the southern tip of the North Island, the castle rocks of the Canterbury foothills that stand alongside the road to Arthur's Pass, and the limestone outcrops of the Rangitikei and King Country districts. Looking at one such outcrop a century ago, the pioneer scholar-poet Edward Tregear wrote:

When Earth was tottering in its infancy,
This rock, a drop of molten stone, was hurled
And tost on waves of flames like those we see
(Distinctly though afar) evolved and whirled
A photosphere of fire around the Solar World.

One of the great tourist attractions of the limestone country of the central North Island is the Waitomo Caves, well known for the grand display provided by the myriads of native glow worms. But no less spectacular are the shape of the caves themselves, the lofty cathedrals of rock that open up in the underground darkness, and the menacing growth of stalactites and stalagmites that bear witness to countless millions of drops of water, impregnated with natural chemicals, dripping unheard through the dark centuries.

Previous page: Thermal terraces, Waimangu, Rotorua, North Island

Right: The Pinnacles, Cape Palliser, Wairarapa, North Island

Below: "Pancake" rocks, Punakaiki, West Coast, South Island

Left: Sand dunes, Otakau, Wanganui, North Island

Below: Limestone outcrops, Castle Hill, Canterbury, South Island

Left: Moeraki boulder, Otago, South Island

Right: Limestone outcrop near Te Anga, King Country, North Island

Below: Rock formation near Cromwell, Otago, South Island

Below: Algal vegetation in a quiescent thermal pool,
Waimangu, Rotorua, North Island

Below: Thermal activity at Hell's Gate or Tikitere, Rotorua,
North Island

Left: Pohutu Geyser erupting, Whakarewarewa, Rotorua, North Island

Below: "A Devil's Ulcer", Waimangu, Rotorua, North Island

Following page: Stalactites, Raukakura Cave, Waitomo, King Country, North Island

'Upon the upland road
Ride easy, stranger:
Surrender to the sky
Your heart of anger.'
JAMES K. BAXTER

The skies over New Zealand are remarkable for their clarity. Visitors accustomed to the foggier air of low-lying continental climates or the more polluted atmosphere of the vast industrial urban sprawls of older countries, find the visual beauty of the New Zealand landscape greatly enhanced by the sharpness with which it can be viewed over long distances.

The New Zealand sky is subject to as many moods as the weather, but it seems to have uniquely crystalline quality, especially at the rising and setting of the sun. And dawns and sunsets derive an intensified splendour from the dramatic forms of the landscape that they illumine or throw into the dark contrast of silhouette.

Mountains, islands, forests, lakes, rocks, mudflats, rivers, harbours and gently crumpled hill country, all take on a fresh and sharper sublimity in the light of the rising sun, or outlined against the splendour of its setting.

It was in such sights that Wordsworth, in another age and place, found

A sense sublime
Of something far more deeply interfused,
Whose dwelling is the light of setting suns,
And the round ocean, and the living air,
And the blue sky, and in the mind of man.

But we need to remind ourselves that skies were more blue, air more living, and sunsets seen with stronger light in the pre-industrial England of Wordsworth, and that perhaps one has to come to New Zealand to recapture that kind of vision that inspired that very English poet.

It was this quality of atmosphere that made Fairburn seek in the wilder extremities of New Zealand's hills for

peace at the heart of strife
and a core of stillness in the whirlwind

and Edward Tregear, watching the sun setting over the Te Whetu Plains, muse like this about life and death:

May age conduct me by a gentle hand,
Beneath the shadows ever brooding o'er
The solemn twilight of the Evening Land,
Where man's discordant voices pierce no more,
But sleeping waters dream along a sleeping shore.

Previous page: Sunset over hill country, Wanganui, North
Island

Left: Tidal flats in Whangarei Harbour at sunset, Northland,
North Island

Below: Clouds catch the setting sun, Motupiko Valley,
Nelson, South Island

Below: Three Kings Islands off the tip of Northland at sundown, North Island

Left: Evening sky near Wellington, North Island

Right: Dusk on a tidal inlet near Motueka, Nelson, South Island

Following page: Looking west towards the Tasman Sea, the Southern Alps in the foreground, with the Fox River in the distance, South Island